BY JENNA TOLLI

I0810816

TAYLOR

AND THE SWIFTIES

EVERYTHING TAYLOR SWIFT

(Gareth's Version)

Gareth Stevens PUBLISHING

Please visit our website, www.garethstevens.com. For a free color catalog of all our high-quality books, call toll free 1-800-542-2595 or fax 1-877-542-2596.

Library of Congress Cataloging-in-Publication Data
Names: Tolli, Jenna, author.
Title: Taylor and the Swifties / Jenna Tolli.
Description: Buffalo, New York : Gareth Stevens Publishing, 2025. | Series: Everything Taylor Swift (Gareth's version) | Includes index.
Identifiers: LCCN 2024027407 | ISBN 9781482469394 (library binding) | ISBN 9781482469387 (paperback) | ISBN 9781482469400 (ebook)
Subjects: LCSH: Swift, Taylor, 1989–Juvenile literature. | Swifties (Music fans)–Juvenile literature.
Classification: LCC ML3930.S989 T65 2025 | DDC 782.421642092–dc23/eng/20240618
LC record available at https://lccn.loc.gov/2024027407

Published in 2025 by
Gareth Stevens Publishing
2544 Clinton Street
Buffalo, NY 14224

Designer: Tanya Dellaccio Keeney
Editor: Kristen Nelson

Special thanks to our favorite Swifties: Charlotte R., for her interview and Nora H., for her help making bracelets.

Photo credits: Series art monicaodo/Shutterstock.com; cover Sipa USA/Alamy Images; cover Imago/Alamy Images; cover, pp. 28, 29 (friendship bracelet) Yuliqwiart/Shutterstock.com; p. 5 corleve/Alamy Images; p. 7 Everett Collection/Shutterstock.com; p. 8 Catrina Haze/Shutterstock.com; p. 9 Terry Murden/Alamy Images; pp. 11, 25 Courtesy of Paolo Villanueva/Flickr.com; p. 15 (top) Dutchmen Photography/Shutterstock.com; p. 15 (bottom) RidhamSupriyanto/Shutterstock.com; p. 16 ChristinaAiko Photography/Shutterstock.com; p. 17 (left) Stefano Chiacchiarini '74/Shutterstock.com; p. 17 (right) melissamn/Shutterstock.com; p. 19 UPI/Alamy Images; p. 21 Brian Friedman/Shutterstock.com; p. 23 Doug Peters/Alamy Images; p. 27 (microphone) AkimD/Shutterstock.com; p. 27 (map) Andrei Minsk/Shutterstock.com; p. 28 (scissors) JuulDu/Shutterstock.com.

Printed in the United States of America

CPSIA compliance information: Batch #CWGS25: For further information contact Gareth Stevens at 1-800-542-2595.

CONTENTS

BOLDFACE WORDS APPEAR IN GLOSSARY

WHO ARE SWIFTIES?

Taylor Swift is one of the most popular artists in the world. She writes songs about what happens in her life, both good and bad. During her **career**, lots of people have connected with the words to her songs, or lyrics, and become fans of her music. There are millions of Taylor Swift fans all around the world. They call themselves Swifties!

Swifties can be any age. Are you a Swiftie? Maybe your parent or teacher is a Swiftie too!

KNOW IT ALL

Did you know that the word Swiftie is trademarked? This means only Taylor can use this word in certain ways.

IN TAYLOR'S WORDS

"My fans came up with a name for themselves, and it's so cute. They call themselves Swifties. And it's adorable 'cause they made it up on their own."
(YouTube, October 29, 2012)

Swifties have been called one of the most loyal, or faithful, fan bases in the world.

EARLY CAREER

Taylor's first three albums, *Taylor Swift* (2006), *Fearless* (2008), and *Speak Now* (2010) are in the country **genre**. She started singing more pop music with her album, *Red* (2012). But with her first official pop album, *1989* (2014), more people started to love her music than ever before!

Many fans of Taylor's like both pop and country music—among other music genres. Taylor has used the sounds of lots of different types of music for her songs, including rock, hip-hop, and folk.

KNOW IT ALL

Taylor has won the Grammy **Award** for album of the year four different times! These awards were for her albums *Fearless*, *1989*, *folklore* (2020), and *Midnights* (2022).

Lots of Swifties have been fans of Taylor's since she was thought of as a country singer.

ONLY THE YOUNG

Some fans have been listening to Taylor Swift since the beginning of her career. But many of her young fans were born after—sometimes long after—her first album came out in 2006.

Charlotte, a Taylor Swift fan born in 2015, started listening to Taylor's music with her mom. She says the age difference between her and Taylor doesn't change how she feels about Taylor's music. "Her songs **inspire** me," she said, naming "Who's Afraid of Little Old Me?" as a favorite. "Me and my friends are Swifties."

IN TAYLOR'S WORDS

"There is an element to my fan base where we feel like we grew up together."
(*Miss Americana*, 2020)

Some fans who started listening to Taylor Swift when her first albums came out are now sharing them with their children. They are inspiring a whole new **generation** of Swifties!

THE CROWDS WENT WILD

Due to the COVID-19 **pandemic**, Taylor and other music artists couldn't tour, or travel doing concerts, for a few years. Swifties were excited to see Taylor in concert again when The Eras Tour kicked off in 2023.

It was hard—and pricey—to get tickets to The Eras Tour. Ticketmaster, a website where people can buy concert tickets, stopped working when tickets went on sale. A lot of people weren't able to get tickets because of this. Swifties spoke out, and they took **legal** action against Ticketmaster.

KNOW IT ALL

Taylor played songs from all of her albums on The Eras Tour. She also included surprise songs at every show!

An average of 72,500 tickets were sold for each show on The Eras Tour. That's a lot of Swifties!

MAKE THE FRIENDSHIP BRACELETS

Fans have long made homemade shirts and outfits for Taylor's concerts to show how much they love her music. Fans have also made signs with song lyrics or messages for Taylor.

In the song "You're on Your Own, Kid," Taylor sings: "So make the friendship bracelets, take the moment and taste it / You've got no reason to be afraid." During The Eras Tour, Swifties started to make their own friendship bracelets in honor of these lyrics!

Sometimes Swifties put a song title or the first letters of each word of a song title on their friendship bracelets. Here are some examples of popular Taylor Swift friendship bracelets.

YOYOK (YOU'RE ON YOUR OWN, KID)

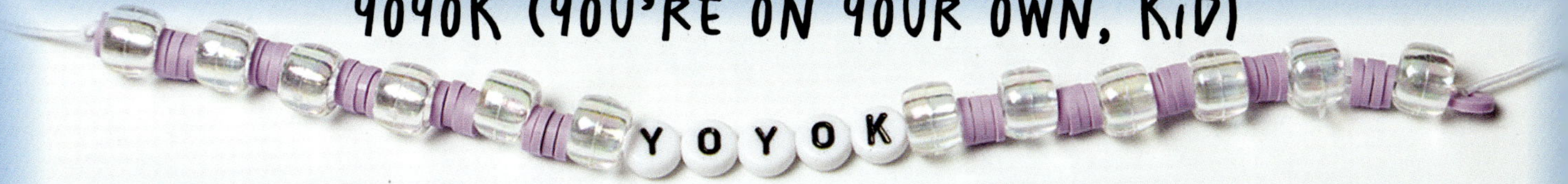

ATWTMV
(ALL TOO WELL
TEN-MINUTE VERSION)

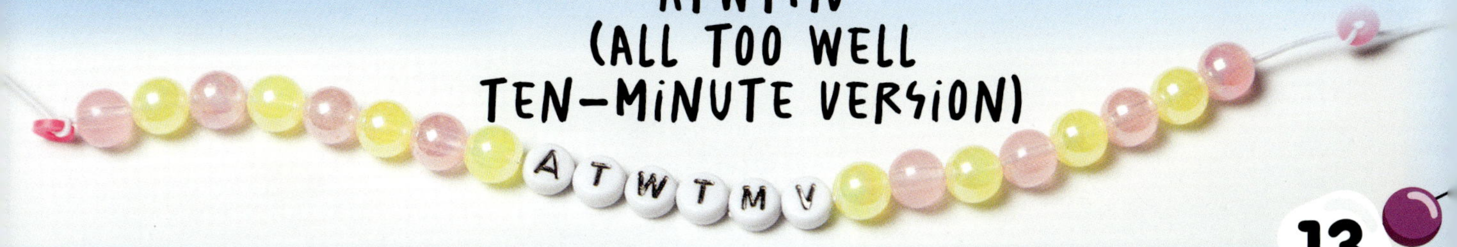

SHOWING SUPPORT

Fans show the world they are Swifties in many ways. Fan websites and accounts on **social media** help Swifties connect with each other. The anonymous, or unknown, owner of the @TSwiftErasTour, a fan account on X, told *Cosmopolitan* in 2024, "I can say that it's even more enjoyable to be a Swiftie now, which is why a lot of people are hopping on the Swiftie train."

Fans also love to wear T-shirts and other clothing that can be bought at tour stops or from Taylor's website.

Swifties can spot each other out and about when wearing something bought at the shop on The Eras Tour, shown here.

TAYLOR SWIFT
THE ERAS TOUR
2023 - 2024
€45

TAYLOR SWIFT
THE ERAS TOUR
OFFICIAL MERCHANDISE

TAYLOR'S VERSION

In recent years, the master recordings from Taylor's first six albums have been sold—and not to Taylor. Since Taylor wrote or co-wrote the songs on these albums, she can rerecord them after a certain period of time. This helps her control how the songs will be used.

The rerecorded albums have the same name and songs on them but include the words "Taylor's Version" after each title. Swifties have stood behind Taylor, choosing to **stream** the new versions instead of the originals.

Taylor releases, or puts out, different copies of her albums with bonus songs and several cool covers. Some Swifties like to collect all the versions, or forms—even if they already own the original!

1989 (ORIGINAL)

YEAR RELEASED
2014

FIRST WEEK SALES
1.287 MILLION

1989 (TAYLOR'S VERSION)

YEAR RELEASED
2023

FIRST WEEK SALES
1.359 MILLION

KNOW IT ALL

A master recording is the official, original recording of a song.

APPRECIATING THE FANS

Taylor values her fans and enjoys connecting with them. She has invited Swifties to secret parties when a new album is about to come out. Here, fans get to hang out with Taylor and hear new songs before anyone else! These secret parties are super special because you can't buy tickets—Taylor's team personally invites fans.

Taylor likes to connect with fans through social media too. Sometimes she surprises them by commenting on their posts or sending personal messages.

KNOW IT ALL

Taylor has donated, or given, money to help fans during hard times in their lives. She has helped them pay for school or hospital bills.

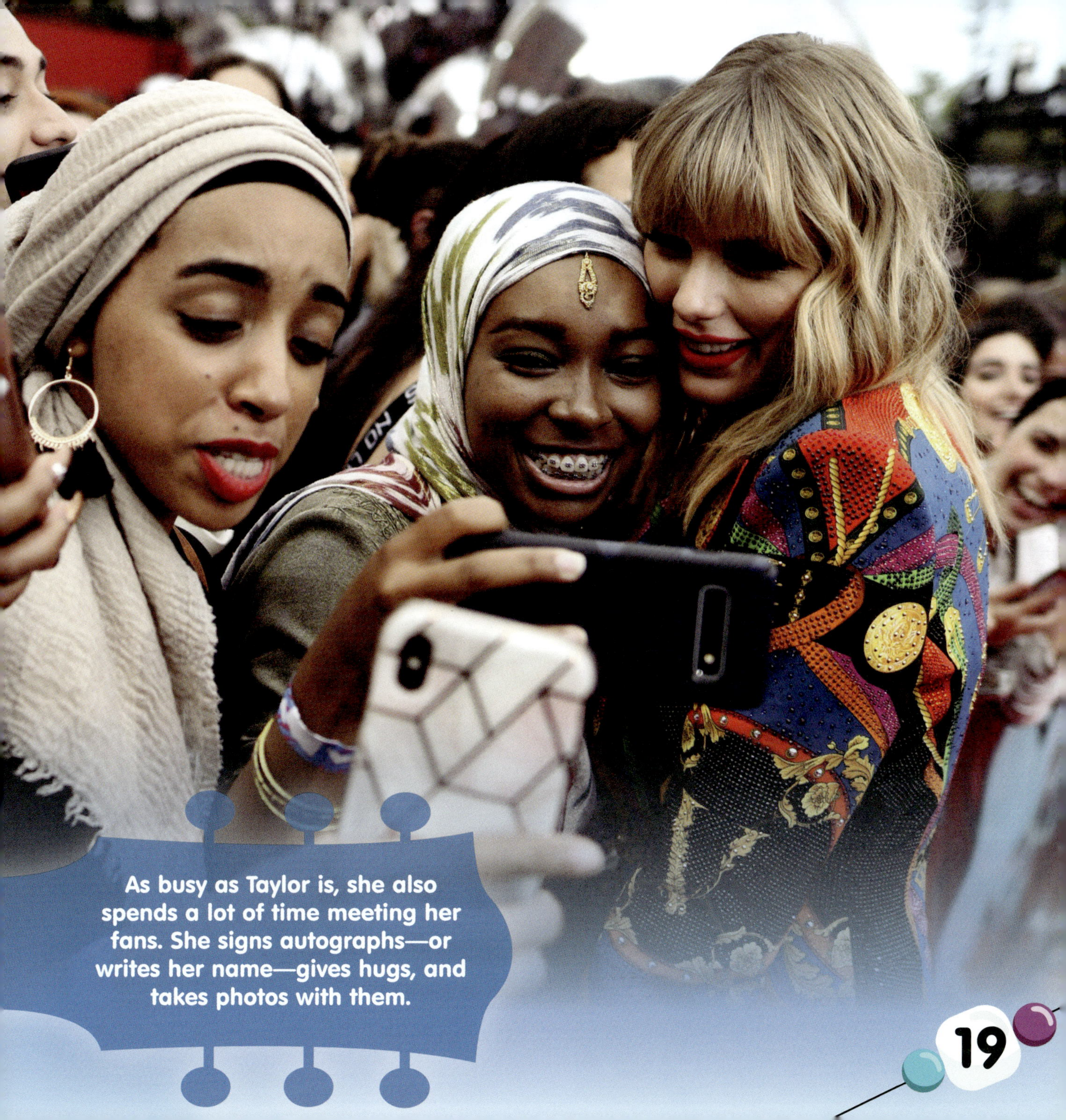

As busy as Taylor is, she also spends a lot of time meeting her fans. She signs autographs—or writes her name—gives hugs, and takes photos with them.

MASTERMIND

Sometimes Taylor includes Easter eggs, or clues, in her work for fans to find. Swifties know to look for these kinds of secret messages. She has added hidden words or messages in her album lyrics sheets by capitalizing certain letters.

She has also given clues at award shows, in the press, and in music videos. On social media, she posts hints about big announcements, such as the date a new album will come out. Swifties share ideas about what the posts could mean.

IN TAYLOR'S WORDS

"I love that [fans] like the **cryptic** hint-dropping. Because as long as they like it, I'll keep doing it. It's fun."
(*Entertainment Weekly*, May 9, 2019)

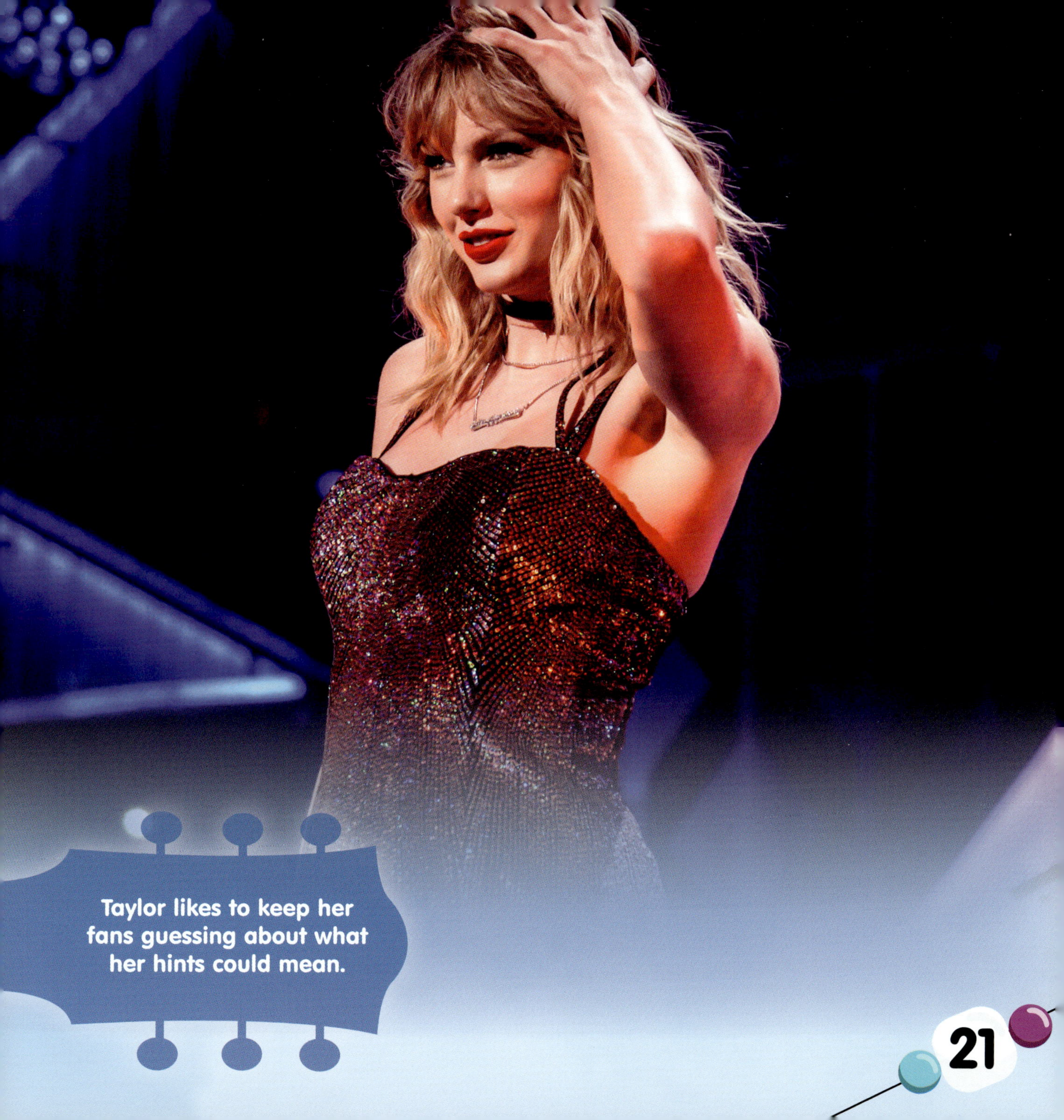

Taylor likes to keep her fans guessing about what her hints could mean.

SWIFTIES MAKING AN IMPACT

When Swifties come together, they can have a big impact, or effect, on the world around them. Taylor knows this and has **encouraged** her fans to vote and speak up about equal rights.

In the music video for "You Need to Calm Down," Taylor introduced fans to the Equality Act. This bill in Congress would make it illegal to **discriminate** against **LGBTQ+** Americans. The video ends with an on-screen message: "Let's show our pride by **demanding** that, on a national level, our laws truly treat all of our citizens equally."

KNOW IT ALL

Taylor started to speak out about equal rights and other ideas that she finds important in 2018.

When Taylor won an award for the "You Need to Calm Down" video, she thanked her fans in her speech.

INSPIRING MUSICIANS

Taylor has inspired a whole generation of new singers and songwriters during her career. Singer and actress Olivia Rodrigo has talked about Taylor's inspiration often. Lots of other musicians—including Maya Hawke—have shared that they've been longtime fans of her music too.

Some artists have been fans and later got to work with Taylor! Singer-songwriter Gracie Abrams told *Teen Vogue* in 2021: "I've always been so inspired at every stage of my life as a fan of hers." On Gracie's 2024 album, Taylor sings on the song "us."!

KNOW-IT-ALL

Olivia Rodrigo has said her hit song "Deja Vu" was inspired by Taylor's song "Cruel Summer."

Some people have been encouraged to write songs or play the guitar—thanks to Taylor.

BIGGER THAN THE WHOLE SKY

Millions of Swifties around the world love Taylor's music and have helped her break records for streaming and music sales. They buy tickets to her shows in record numbers and enjoy following her career as it grows to new heights. People who have grown up listening to Taylor have even been inspired to make music of their own.

Swifties are so excited to see what Taylor has planned for the future. Long live all the magic Taylor has made!

Taylor toured all over the world in 2023 and 2024 on The Eras Tour. In addition to the United States, the tour visited countries like Mexico, Japan, Australia, and Spain.

THE ERAS TOUR (2023–2024)

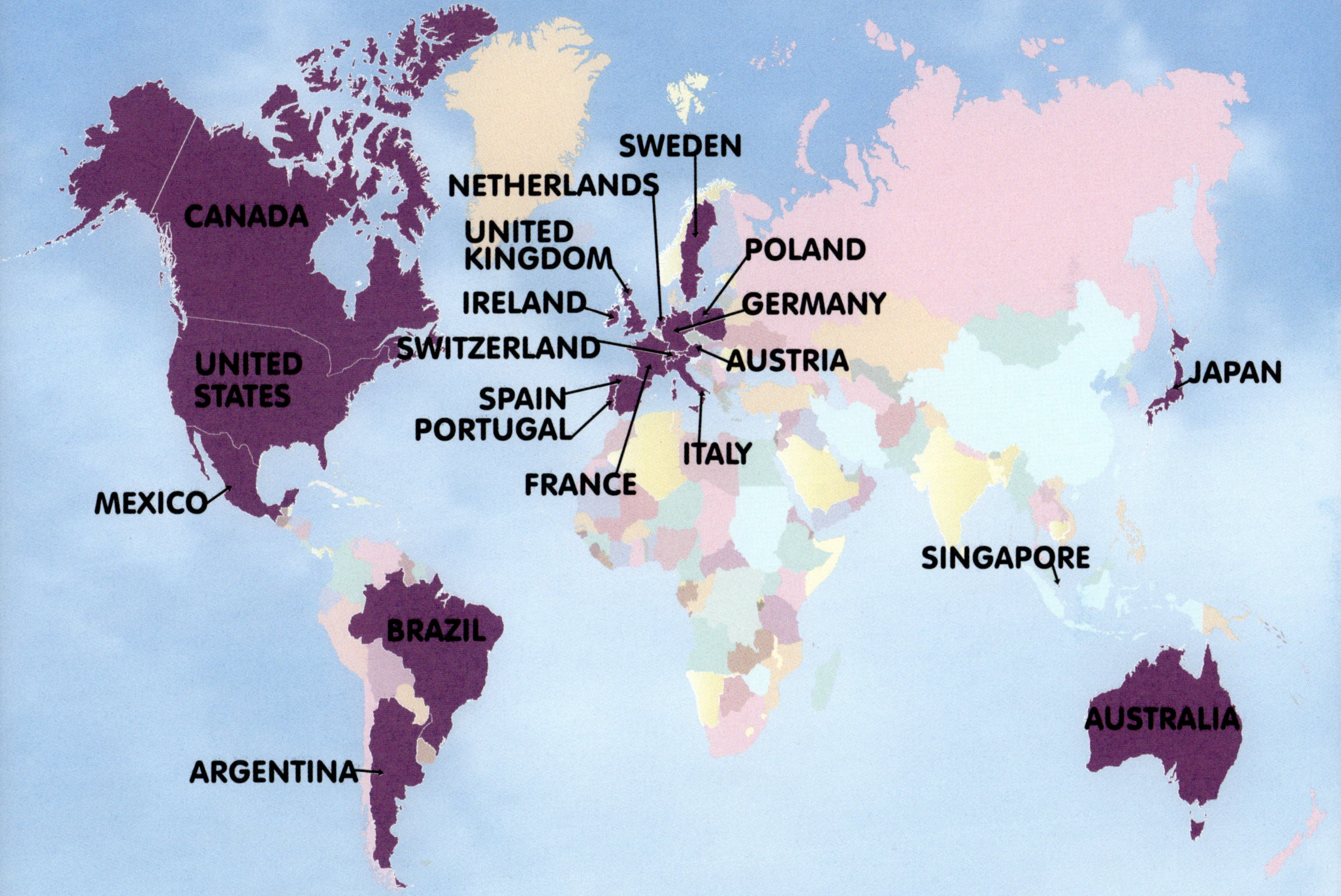

COUNTRIES TAYLOR VISITED ON THE ERAS TOUR

ACTIVITY: MAKE FRIENDSHIP BRACELETS

Swifties made and wore bracelets like these during The Eras Tour! Make some for yourself or your friends following these simple steps.

MATERIALS

- thin, stretchy string (be sure it's thin enough to fit through all the kinds of beads you buy)
- colored beads
- letter beads
- shape beads (stars, hearts, flowers, etc.)
- scissors

STEPS

STEP 1

Cut the string. Make it about 12 inches (30.5 cm) in length.

STEP 2

Tie a knot at one end of the bracelet. If you need help with this, ask an adult or friend. You can also tape one end of the string to a table to keep beads from slipping off as you make your bracelet.

STEP 3

Plan your bracelet. Start with a colored bead (or several) and then make a word. This can be the name or first letters of your favorite Taylor Swift song, your favorite lyric, a word, or your name! Use a blank bead for spaces between words.

STEP 4

String your colored beads and letter beads onto the bracelet. Add more colored beads at the end.

STEP 5

Wrap the bracelet around your wrist. Tie the ends together, pulling it close to your wrist so it won't fall off. Trim off leftover string. Wear it with pride or give it to a friend!

GLOSSARY

award: A prize given for doing something.

career: The job someone chooses to do for a long time.

cryptic: Meant to be puzzling or mysterious.

demand: To say strongly that something must happen.

discriminate: To treat a person or group of people unfairly and differently from other people or groups.

encourage: To tell someone to do something.

generation: A group of people born about the same time.

genre: A type or style of music, such as country or rap.

inspire: To cause someone to want to do something.

legal: Having to do with the law.

LGBTQ+: Stands for the lesbian, gay, bisexual, transgender and queer community.

pandemic: A time when a disease, or sickness, spreads quickly and affects many people in a place or throughout the world.

social media: Websites and applications, also known as apps, used to create online communities.

stream: To transfer data in a continuous way, meant to be watched or listened to immediately.

FOR MORE INFORMATION

Books

Kawa, Katie. *Taylor Swift: Making a Difference as a Songwriter*. New York, New York: KidHaven Publishing, 2022.

Rose, Rachel. *Taylor Swift: Singer, Songwriter, and Activist.* Minneapolis, Minnesota: Bearport Publishing Company, 2023.

Websites

Billboard: Taylor Swift
https://www.billboard.com/artist/taylor-swift/
Explore the latest news about Taylor Swift and check out her most popular songs.

Taylor Swift
www.taylorswift.com/
Learn more about Taylor Swift on her official website.

Publisher's note to educators and parents: Our editors have carefully reviewed these websites to ensure that they are suitable for students. Many websites change frequently, however, and we cannot guarantee that a site's future contents will continue to meet our high standards of quality and educational value. Be advised that students should be closely supervised whenever they access the internet.

INDEX